Flavors of

THAI
Cooking

Inspired by STAR TV Shows

Contents

Introduction

The Eastern and Western influences have caused the development of a rich and varied cuisine, using mainly fish and seafood from the coast, meat from inland as well as a variety of new ingredients leading to the genesis of the renowned Thai cuisine. The Chinese, Portuguese, Dutch, French and Japanese have all left their impact on Thai cooking.

Initially seafood and herbs were the major ingredients, as the Thais abhorred the use of meat owing to their Buddhist beliefs. The Chinese introduced frying, stir frying and deep frying to Thai cooking which was more accustomed to the methods of stewing, baking and grilling. The Thais began using Chilies after the late 1600's. They were good at altering foreign cooking methods and replacing the ingredients of traditional recipes, coming up with their very own kind. Ghee was substituted with coconut oil and pungent spices gave way to milder ones. Fresh herbs like lemon grass and galanga were extensively used. A special feature of Thai cuisine is that instead of going by courses, food is served all at once giving diners the opportunity to relish a fusion of tastes. Single-dish meals like 'khao phat' and 'thai phat' are popular.

A Thai meal is well balanced. A typical meal consists of a clear soup, a steamed dish, a fried dish, a hot salad and a variety of dips. Each dish is in accordance with the other as the spicy items can be replaced with non-spicy ones if required. In case the soup is spicy the curry dish can be substituted with non-spicy items to allow each dish to agree with each other. Thai meals are unique blends of spicy, mild, sweet and sour flavours.

Lemon grass, galanga, kaffir lime leaves and fish sauce are some of the extensively used items. They form the ingredients of salad dressings, soup stocks, curries, dips and single-dish meals as well.

Tidbits or hors d'oeuvres are accessories served with the main dish. Spring rolls, satay and puffed rice cakes with herbed toppings are some examples of tidbits.

Basic stocks of common Thai soups can be made by adding crushed peppercorns, salt, garlic, shallots, coriander roots and meat to boiling water. Thai soups combined with rice constitute a full meal. Traditional Thai soups are special in the sense that they incorporate more flavours and textures that are found in other foodstuffs.

The common dip to go with any Thai dish can be made by mixing crushed fresh Chilies with fish sauce and a dash of lime. This can be made into an all purpose dip or 'nam phrik' by adding some crushed garlic with a little raw shrimp paste. Dips can be served with steamed rice, an omelette and vegetables.

Salad dressings that go with boiled, grilled or fried meat can be made by mixing lemon grass, galanga and shallots with dips. This can be garnished with lettuce leaves, sliced cucumber, cut spring onions and coriander leaves.

Curry pastes which form the base of Thai curries can be made by combining Chilies, garlic, shallots, galanga, lemon grass, coriander roots, ground pepper, kaffir lime peels and shrimp paste. Curries can be seasoned with fish sauce, sugar and coconut milk and garnished with sliced eggplant, basil and kaffir lime leaves. Thai curries might be hot or even bland. Hot Thai curies are known to burn but the taste doesn't stay for long.

Thai meals are concluded with desserts or fresh fruits like mangoes, durian, jackfruit, papaya, grapes or melon.

Thai cuisine boasts of an unequalled ability to adapt to new influences and alter it according to their own terms resulting in a remarkable harmony of tastes and flavours.

Sour & Spicy Chicken Soup

(Tom Yum Gai)

Serves: 4
Cooking time (approx.): 25–30 minutes

Ingredients:

Boneless chicken (shredded)	: 400 gms	Kaffir lime leaves	: 2–3
Chicken stock	: 4 cups	Fish sauce	: 3 tbsp
Mushrooms (cut)	: 100 gms	Fresh lime juice	: 4 tbsp
Cherry tomatoes (halved)	: 6	Sugar	: ½ tsp
Lemongrass	: 1 stalk	Red chilies	: 6–8

Procedure:

1) In a pot, take the chicken stock, lemongrass and lime leaves and bring to a boil.

2) As the soup boils, add the chicken shreds, mushrooms, fish sauce, lime juice and sugar and cook until the chicken becomes tender. Simmer.

3) After the chicken becomes white, add the cherry tomatoes and the red chilies and simmer for 10–15 minutes.

4) Serve hot.

Tip:

- The soup tastes best with jasmine rice. You can also replace the chicken with the meat of your choice.

Coconut Seafood Soup

Serves: 3–4

Cooking time: 35 minutes

Ingredients:

Coconut milk	: 3 cups	Onion (quartered and sliced)	: 1 small
Lemongrass	: 2 stalks	Red jalapeño	: 3–4
Fresh Galanga	: 2–3" pieces	Fresh mushrooms	: 2 cups
Prawns	: 8 medium	Fish sauce	: 4–6 tbs
Salt	: ½ tsp	Lime juice	: 5 tsp
Squid (whole)	: 4–5	Palm sugar	: 1–2 tbs
Mussels (shelled)	: 8–10	White pepper (freshly ground)	: ¼ tsp
Baking soda	: ½ tsp	Cilantro leaves	: 6–8
Crab	: ½		
Sea scallops	: 8		

Procedure:

1) Slice and smash the galanga and lemongrass and put in a soup pot.

2) Divide the coconut milk into two halves and dilute one half with 3 cups of water. Add this to the pot and bring to a boil. Then simmer for about 15 minutes.

3) Meanwhile, shell out the seafood and add salt and baking soda. Keep aside for 10 minutes. Rinse thoroughly with water.

4) Now add the onion, jalapeño and white pepper to the soup. Simmer again for 2–3 minutes.

5) In the pot add the mushrooms and the remaining coconut cream and stir well.

6) As the soup begins to boil, first add the mussels and crab followed by the remaining seafood. Now add the fish sauce.

7) Add the sugar and lime as per your taste.
8) Remove from heat and serve. Garnish with fresh cilantro leaves.

Tip:
- Use lots of galanga for a rich taste.

Hot & Sour Seafood Soup

(Tom Yum Taleh)

Serves: 2

Cooking time (approx.): 15 minutes

Ingredients:			
Water	: 3 cups	Mackerel	: 1 medium
Fresh tomato (sliced)	: 2 medium	Shrimp	: 1 medium
Lemongrass (freshly cut):	2–3 pieces	Lime juice	: 5–6 tsp
Garlic cloves (crushed)	: 2–3	Red Chilies	: 4–5
Sea salt	: 2 tsp	Fish sauce as per taste	
Whole squid	: 2 small		

Procedure:

1) Clean and slice the seafood.

2) In a pot, add water, lemongrass, garlic and sea salt. Bring to a boil for 3–4 minutes.

3) Now add the squid and fish. Boil for another 2 minutes.

4) Add the rest of the seafood along with the lime juice, red Chilies and fish sauce. Mix well.

5) Now put in the tomato slices. Simmer for 5 minutes and remove from heat.

Tip:

• This soup tastes best when served alongside Jasmine rice.

Thai Chicken & Rice Soup

Serves: 4–6
Cooking time (approx.): 20 minutes

Ingredients:

Chicken broth	: 6 cups	Bamboo shoots (cut)	: ½ cup
Raw chicken		Whole red Chilies	: 2
breast (sliced)	: 1–2	Fish sauce	: 4 tbsp
Ginger (grated)	: 1" piece	Lime juice	: 4 tsp
Garlic cloves (crushed)	: 3	Coconut milk	: ½ cup
Celery (sliced)	: 1 stalk	Brown sugar	: 1 tsp
Mushrooms (sliced)	: 1 cup	Spring onions (sliced)	: 2
Thai rice (cooked)	: 1 cup	Coriander	: for
Mini corn cobs (sliced)	: ½ cup		garnishing

Procedure:

1) Put the chicken into the broth and boil for about 10 minutes.

2) Add the ginger, garlic, celery and mushrooms to the pot and boil on a medium flame for another 2–3 minutes.

3) Stirring continuously, add the rice, corn cobs, bamboo shoots and chilly. Simmer for 2 minutes.

4) Now put the coconut milk, fish sauce, sugar and lime juice. Stir well to blend the things together. Add the ingredients as per your taste.

5) Before removing from heat, add the fresh spring onions.

6) Garnish with coriander leaves and serve hot.

Tip:

• If you're using uncooked rice, use an extra cup of chicken stock and boil the rice in it. Then continue as usual.

Sour & Spicy Lemongrass Shrimp Soup

(Tom Yum Goong)

Serves: 3–4

Cooking time (approx.): 20 minutes

Ingredients:

Water	: 4 cups	Shrimps	: 2 medium
Lemongrass (fresh and sliced)	: 2 stalks	Chilly peppers	: 12
		White onion (sliced)	: 1
Ginger (fresh and sliced)	: 3 one" slices	Roasted chilly paste	: 2 tbsp
		Mushrooms	: ½ cup
		Tomato (chopped)	: 1
Tamarind paste	: 1 tbsp	Lime juice	: 4 tbsp
Fish sauce	: 1 tbsp	Cilantro	: 2 sprigs

Procedure:

1) In a soup pot, boil the water and add the lemongrass, ginger, tamarind paste and fish sauce.

2) Shell and de–vein the shrimps and add to the pot. Boil for 3 minutes.

3) Add the sliced onions, roasted chilly paste and the mushrooms and boil for another 8 minutes.

4) Add the chilly peppers and the tomatoes. Remove from heat and add the lime juice.

5) Add the fish sauce and garnish with cilantro leaves.

6) Serve hot.

Tip:

- You can substitute the shrimps with firm white– flesh fish or even chicken.

Chicken Noodle Soup

Ingredients:

Fresh Chicken Breast (chopped)	: 1–2	Fresh lime juice	: ¼ cup
Chicken Broth	: 6 cups	Fish sauce	: 1–3 tbsp
Lemongrass	: 1 stalk	Coconut milk	: ¼ cup
Carrot (sliced)	: 1 large	Black pepper as per taste	
Red Chilies (sliced)	: 1–2	Fresh basil leaves	: 6–8
Garlic Cloves (minced)	: 3	Dry flat Thai rice noodles	: 500 gms
Ginger	: 1" piece	Sugar (optional)	: 1–2 tsp

Procedure:

1) Soak the noodles in hot water for 10 minutes and then rinse with cold water to avoid stickiness.

2) Bring the chicken broth to a boil. Add the garlic, ginger, lemongrass and red Chilies.

3) Add the fresh chicken pieces and continue boiling for about 10 minutes.

4) Add the fish sauce and carrots and simmer.

5) Now add the coconut milk and stir continuously. Put the lime juice, black pepper and sugar.

6) Pour the soup over a bowl of noodles. Garnish with fresh basil leaves.

Seafood Salad

(Yam Talay)

Serves: 3–4

Cooking time (approx.): 20 minutes

Ingredients:

Crab meat	: 150 gms	Melted palm sugar	: 1 tsp
Squid (cut into pieces)	: 150 gms	Lemongrass	: 3 lower stalks
Mussles (meat only)	: 50 gms		
Fish fillet (cut)	: 50 gms	Onion medium (sliced)	: ½
Prawns	: 100 gms	Tomato (sliced)	: 1
Fish sauce	: 4 tbsp	Celery (roughly chopped)	: ½ cup
Lime juice	: 5 tbsp	Spring onions (chopped)	: 4
Green Chilies (chopped)	: 20 small		

Procedure:

1) In a pan, boil some water. Cook the prawns, crab, squid, mussles and fish separately. When cooked, mix all the seafood together.

2) In a bowl, mix the fish sauce, lime juice, melted palm sugar and green Chilies.

3) To this mixture, add the seafood and mix well. Now add the lemongrass.

4) Now add the onion, tomato, celery and spring onions.

5) Toss and serve.

Note :

- Cook the seafood separately and only then mix them together

Cucumber Salad

Serves: 4
Cooking time (approx.): 5–10 minutes

Ingredients:

Sweet red bell peppers	: ½	Sea salt	: ¼ tsp
Cucumbers	: 4	Sugar	: 2 tbsp
Shallots (chopped)	: 2	Vinegar	: ⅓ cup
Coriander (finely chopped)	: 1 tbsp		

Procedure:

1) Wash the cucumbers and slice.
2) In a pan, mix vinegar, salt and sugar and simmer until the mixture turns into a syrupy sauce. Remove from heat and allow to cool.
3) Mix the cucumbers, shallots and bell peppers together.
4) Pour the cold sauce over the vegetables and garnish with coriander leaves.

Tip:
- Serve this cooling salad alongside Chicken satay.

Spicy Eggplant Salad

Serves: 6–8

Cooking time (approx.): 20 minutes

Ingredients:

Long eggplants	: 4	Fresh shrimp (small)	: 1
Jalapeno	: 4	Hard– boiled egg (cut	
Thai Chilies	: 10–15	into small wedges)	: 1
Lime juice	: 4–6 tsp	Cilantro sprigs	: 6–8
Fish sauce	: 2–3 tbsp		
Sugar	: 2–3 tsp		
Shallots (cleaned and			
de–veined)	: 2		

Procedure:

1) Grill the eggplants and jalapeno in an electric grill or charcoal grill turning occasionally.
2) Mix the Chilies, fish sauce, lime juice and sugar to make a hot– and– sour sauce.
3) Blanch the shrimps in boiling water and then drain.
4) Remove the charred skin from the eggplants and jalapenos and slice.
5) Place the slices onto a platter and place the shrimps and shallots on top.
6) Spread the sauce evenly over the salad.
7) Garnish with egg wedges and cilantro sprigs.

Tip:
• Serve with chicken or other protein.

Spicy Minced Chicken Salad with Mint and Toasted Rice

(Laab Gai)

Serves: 1–2

Cooking time (approx.): 15–20 minutes

Ingredients:

Boneless chicken (chopped): 150 gms		Dried Thai Chilies	: 2–4 tsp
Peanut oil	: 1 tbsp	Fish sauce	: 3 tbsp
Garlic (minced and formed into a paste)	: 6	Lime juice	: 6 tsp
		Sugar	: 1 tsp
Lemongrass (chopped)	: 1 stalk	Roasted rice (ground)	: 2 tbsp
Shallot (chopped)	: 1	Assortment of raw or lightly steamed vegetables	
Green onions (chopped)	: 2		
Fresh mint leaves	: ½ cup		
Ginger	: 2 small pieces		

Procedure:

1) Cook the chicken in the oil until thoroughly cooked.

2) Toast the ginger and Thai Chilies in a dry pan until it begins to char and then dry grind into a fine powder.

3) In a bowl mix garlic, mint leaves, lemongrass, shallot and green onions.

4) Toss the cooked chicken with the mixture and the ginger and chilly powder.

5) Now add the fish sauce, lime juice and sugar and mix well.

6) Finally add the roasted rice and mix.

7) Serve alongside a tray of steamed vegetables.

Tip:

• This salad is generally very spicy, but you can add or subtract as per your taste.

Thai Summer Rolls

Serves: 4

Cooking time (approx.): 25 minutes

Ingredients:

Spring roll wrappers (Rice paper)	: 1 pkt.	Dried rice noodles	: 100 gms
Chicken (cut lengthwise)	: 1 cup	Fresh basil	: ½ cup
Honey	: ¼ cup	Fresh coriander	: 1 cup
Fish sauce	: 2 tbsp	Lettuce (chopped)	: 2 cups
Lime juice	: 1 tbsp	Spring onions (sliced lengthwise)	: 4
Chilly sauce	: 2–4 tbsp	Vegetable oil to fry	
White wine	: ¼ cup		

Procedure:

1) Marinate the chicken with honey, fish sauce, lime juice and chilly sauce. Keep aside.

2) Soak the noodles in hot water for 10 minutes. Drain and rinse with cold water.

3) In a pan, heat some oil and add the marinated chicken. To this, add the white wine 1–2 tbsp at a time.

4) Mix together the fresh basil, spring onion, coriander and lettuce in a bowl. Add the cooked chicken as well.

5) In a bowl of hot water, gently dip the rice paper and allow it to soak for about 30 seconds. This will make it soft.

6) On the rice paper, spread a layer of noodles and the chicken–lettuce mixture and fold from all sides.

7) Enjoy with a dipping sauce.

Note:

• These rolls taste best when refrigerated for a couple of hours.

Thai Spring Rolls

Serves: 2–4
Cooking time (approx.): 20 minutes

Ingredients:

Spring roll sheets	: 300 gms	Light soy sauce	: 1½ tbsp
Glass noodles	: 25 gms	Garlic (chopped)	: 1 tbsp
Shredded cabbage	: 1 cup	Rice flour	: 50 gms
White pepper (ground)	: ¼ tsp	Vegetable oil for frying	
Been sprouts	: 1 cup		

Procedure:

1) Mix the rice flour with water and bring to a boil to thicken. Keep aside.
2) Soak the noodles in water for 10 minutes. Drain and cut into pieces.
3) To the noodles add been sprouts, cabbage, pepper and soy sauce.
4) In a pan, fry the garlic until golden– yellow and then mix the noodle mixture to it. Stir fry for a minute.
5) Roll out a spring roll sheet and put a spoonful mixture into the middle. Now close its sides into a cylindrical shape using the rice flour paste.
6) Fry the spring rolls in hot oil until a golden crust forms on top.

To serve: Serve hot with sauce.

Tip:
• If using spring roll wrappers instead, don't use the flour paste.

Chicken Satay

(Gai Satay)

Serves: 4

Cooking time (approx.): 15–20 minutes

(Excludes preparation time)

Ingredients:

Boneless chicken breast	: 500 gms	Ginger	: ¼" piece
Whole coriander seeds	: 1 tsp	Garlic clove (smashed)	: 1
Whole cumin seeds	: 1 tsp	Sea salt	: ½ tsp
Turmeric (ground)	: 1 tsp	Sugar	: 2 tsp
Shallots (peeled and		Bamboo skewers	: 20
sliced)	: 3–4	Cooking oil	: 2 tbsp
Fresh lemongrass	: 1 stalk		

Procedure:

1) In a pan, dry roast the coriander and cumin seeds and then pound using a mortar and pestle. Keep aside.
2) Slice the chicken into medium sized pieces.
3) Marinate the chicken with the spices, ginger, garlic, shallots, turmeric and lemongrass. Keep overnight.
4) Before cooking, soak the bamboo shoots in water to avoid them from burning.
5) Put 3 chicken pieces onto each skewer and grill.

To serve: Serve with sticky rice and cucumber salad.

Thai Egg Rolls

(Po–Pia Thot)

Serves: 6–8

Cooking time (approx.): 20 minutes

Ingredients:

Glass noodles	: 100 gms	Mushrooms (chopped)	: ½ cup (pre soaked)
Egg roll sheets	: 500 gms		
Bean sprouts	: 100 gms	Black pepper	: ½ tbsp
Minced chicken	: 200 gms.	Thai soy sauce	: 1 tbsp
Egg	: 1	Sea salt	: 2 tsp
Cabbage (shredded)	: ½ cup	Garlic (chopped)	: 1 tbsp
Carrot (shredded)	: ½ cup	Cooking oil	: 3 cups

Procedure:

1) Soak the noodles in water and then cut them into small pieces.
2) To the noodles, add egg, cabbage, chicken, carrot, mushroom, pepper, salt and soy sauce and mix well.
3) Fry some garlic in a pan. When golden in colour, add the noodle mixture and toss for bout 2 minutes.
4) In an egg roll sheet, place a serving of this mixture and seal the sides.
5) Deep fry in a pan until crispy brown colour.

To serve: Serve hot.

Tip:

• For best taste, serve with sliced cucumber and sweet basil leaves.

Chinese Chive Dumplings

Serves: 2–4

Cooking time (approx.): 15 minutes

Ingredients:			
Water	: ½ cups	Rice flour	: 1 cup
Vegetable oil	: ¼ cup	Chinese chives (green)	: 2 cups
Refined Flour (maida)	: ¼ cup	Soy sauce	: 1 tbsp
Sticky rice flour	: ¼ cup	Hot chilly sauce	: 1 tbsp

Procedure:

1) Mix rice flour and sticky rice flour in a pot and continue adding water until the mixture becomes a gluey paste.

2) Heat for 2 minutes and add the refined flour. Keep aside for cooling.

3) Slice the chives into ½" pieces.

4) Heat 2 tbsp oil and saute the chives. Now add the soy sauce and hot chilly sauce.

5) Stuff this mixture into the flour paste and seal them.

6) Steam the balls for 7–10 minutes.

7) Your steaming dumplings are ready!

Thai Crab Curry

Serves: 4

Cooking time (approx.): 20 minutes

Ingredients:

Crab	: 1 large	Thai curry powder	: 2 tsp
White onion	: 1	Milk	: ½ cup
Chinese celery	: 2	Roasted chilly paste	: 1 tbsp
Spring onions	: 3	Egg	: 1
Red chilies	: 2	Oyster sauce	: 2 tbsp
White pepper (ground)	: ¼ tsp	Vegetable oil for frying	

Procedure:

1) Wash the crab and remove the shell. Cut into small pieces.
2) In a pan, add 2 tbsp of oil and fry the crab in it until golden brown.
3) Now add the curry powder and mix well.
4) In a bowl, mix the milk, chilly paste and beaten egg.
5) Pour this mixture onto the crab.
6) Now add the oyster sauce.
7) Chop the white onion, celery, spring onions and red chilies and put into the mixture.
8) Mix well. Sprinkle the pepper powder and cook until done.
9) Serve hot.

Note:

- You can replace the crab with scallops, fish or even vegetables or cottage cheese.

Thai Yellow Curry Chicken

(Kaeng Kari Kai)

Serves: 4

Cooking time (approx.): 20 minutes

Ingredients:

Chicken	: 500 gms	**For yellow curry paste:**	
Yellow curry paste	: 2 tbsp	Dried chilies (soaked)	: 3
Potatoes (boiled & peeled)	: 3	Shallots (broiled)	: 5
Coconut milk	: 3 cups	Garlic cloves (broiled)	: 10
Coconut cream	: 1 cup	Ginger (sliced)	: 1 tsp
Shallots (fried)	: 2 tbsp	Lemongrass	: 1 tbsp
Sea salt	: 1 tsp	Coriander seeds (dry roasted)	: 1 tbsp
Vegetable oil	: 2 tbsp	Cumin seeds (dry roasted)	: 1 tsp
		Curry powder	: 2 tsp
		Sea salt	: 1 tsp
		Thai shrimp paste	: 1 tsp

Procedure for chicken:

1) Wash and cut the chicken into pieces. Also dice the potatoes.
2) Fry the curry paste in oil, adding the coconut cream at regular intervals.
3) Cook for 5–8 minutes and then add the chicken.
4) As the chicken becomes tender, put the coconut milk and salt.
5) Stir occasionally. Now add the diced potatoes.
6) Garnish with fried shallots and serve.

Procedure for yellow curry paste:

1) Using a grinder, grind all the ingredients to form a fine powder. This powder can be refrigerated up to 3 weeks.

Tip:

• Serve with cucumber salad. The chicken could also be replaced with cottage cheese or tofu.

Green Curry with Chicken

Serves: *3–4*

Cooking time (approx.): *20 minutes*

(Excludes preparation time)

Ingredients:

Chicken (sliced)	: 400 gms	**For Green Curry Paste (Nam Prik Kaeng Khiaw Waan):**	
Green curry paste	: 3 tbsp		
Coconut milk	: 2 ½ cups	Fresh green hot chilies	: 15 large
Fresh eggplants	: 5 small	Onions (sliced)	: 3
Red chilies (sliced)	: 4–5	Garlic cloves	: 9
Kaffir lime leaves	: 2	Ginger (finely sliced)	: 1 tsp
Sweet basil leaves	: ¼ cup	Lemongrass (sliced)	: 1 tbsp
Fish sauce	: 1½ tbsp	Kaffir lime rind (finely sliced)	: 9 tsp
Palm sugar	: 1½ tsp	Coriander (chopped)	: 1 tsp
Cooking oil	: 1 tbsp	White peppercorns	: 5
		Roasted coriander seeds	: 1 tbsp
		Roasted cumin seeds	: 1 tsp
		Sea salt	: 1 tsp
		Shrimp paste	: 1 tsp

Procedure for Chicken:

1) On a medium flame, sauté the green curry paste.
2) Keeping 1 cup coconut milk aside, add the rest into the pan and stir continuously.
3) Add the chicken slices and the kaffir lime leaves and bring to a boil.
4) When the chicken becomes tender, add the remaining coconut milk, palm sugar and fish sauce. Again bring to a boil.
5) Now add the eggplants and stir.
6) Sprinkle the sweet basil leaves and red chilies and remove from flame.
7) Serve with steamed rice.

Procedure for Green Curry Paste:

1) Combine all the ingredients together except the shrimp paste into a mortar and pound.

2) Now add the shrimp paste and blend into a smooth paste.

Note:

- You can replace the chicken with vegetables, cottage cheese or tofu.

Panang Curry

(Panang Neua)

Ingredients:

Chicken	: 400 gms	Salt	: ¼ tsp
Panang curry paste	: 3 tbsp	Palm sugar	: 3 tbsp
Coconut milk	: 2 cups	Fish sauce	: 2 ½ tbsp
Kaffir lime leaves	: 6	Fresh red chilies for garnishing	
Roasted peanuts (ground)	: ¼ cup		

Procedure:

1) Clean the chicken and dice into pieces.

2) Heat 1 cup of coconut oil in a pan until the oil separates from the milk.

3) Add the curry paste and stir for 2 minutes. Put in the chicken dices and cook until chicken becomes tender.

4) Now pour in the remaining coconut milk. Bring to a boil.

5) Season with salt, sugar and fish sauce. Add roasted peanuts and torn kaffir leaves.

6) Remove from heat and garnish with sliced red chilies.

Roasted Duck curry with Red Curry Paste

Serves: 6

Cooking time (approx.): 15–20 minutes

Ingredients:

Roasted duck (deboned and cut)	: 1 medium	Sugar	: 1 tsp
Coconut milk	: 3 cups	Sea salt	: ½ tsp
Cherry tomatoes	: 10	Thai fish sauce	: 2 tbsop
Eggplant (cut)	: 1 cup	Water/ Chicken stock	: ½ cup
Pineapple (cut)	: 6 pieces	Vegetable oil	: 2 tbsp
		Red curry paste	: 3 tbsp

Procedure:

1) Heat oil in a pan and add 1 cup coconut milk in it. Bring to a boil.
2) Put the curry paste and mix thoroughly.
3) Add the duck and pour in the remaining coconut milk and boil.
4) As the oil begins to come to the surface, add the chicken stock, tomatoes, eggplant, pineapple, sugar, salt, fish sauce and stir regularly.
5) Cook for 5–10 minutes and remove from heat.

Red Curry with Chicken and Bamboo Shoots

Serves: 5

Cooking time (approx.): 20–25 minutes

Ingredients:

Chicken breast	: 500 gms	**For red curry paste:**	
Bamboo shoots (sliced)	: 1 can	Dried red hot	
Red curry paste	: 3 tbsp	chilly peppers	: 25–30
Coconut milk	: 2 cups	Sea salt	: 1 tbsp
Red chilly (sliced)	: 2	Garlic cloves (peeled)	: 4
Sweet basil leaves	: ½ cup	Fresh lemongrass	: 2–3 stalks
Fish sauce	: 2 tbsp	Shrimp paste	: 2–3 tbsp
Sea salt	: ¼ tsp	Turmeric	: ¼" piece
Palm sugar	: 1 ½ tsp		
Sweet basil leaves for garnishing			

Procedure for chicken:

1) Clean and cut the chicken pieces.

2) Put 1 cup coconut milk in the pan and bring to a boil.

3) Add the red curry paste and heat until the oil separates from the mixture.

4) Put in the chicken pieces and sauté until it loses its pink colour.

5) Add the remaining coconut milk and bamboo shoots. Stir.

6) Now add the basil leaves, salt, sugar, fish sauce and the red chilies. Bring to a boil.

7) Garnish with sweet basil leaves before serving.

Procedure for red curry paste:

1) Using a blender, mix all the ingredients together, adding the shrimp paste right in the end to form a smooth paste.

Tip:

• Serve with Jasmine rice.

Shrimp Curry with Choo–Chee

Curry Paste

(Choo CHee Gkung)

Serves: 4–5

Cooking time (approx.): 15–20 minutes

(Excludes preparation time)

Ingredients:

Shrimps or Prawns	: 500 gms	Peanut oil	: 1 tbsp
Mushrooms	: 250 gms	Fish sauce	: 2–3 tbsp
Coconut cream	: 1 cup	Coconut sugar	: 2–3 tsp
Red jalapeno	: 3	Kaffir lime leaves	: 10
Dried red chilies (soaked)	: 7–10	Cilantro	: few
Garlic cloves	: 12–15		sprigs
Shallots (chopped)	: 4–6		
Shrimp paste	: 2 tsp		

Procedure:

1) Shell the shrimp and pour a mixture of water and salt over it. Keep aside for 15–20 minutes. Rinse thoroughly to remove all salt.

2) In a blender, mix the dried red chilies, red jalapenos, garlic cloves, shallots and shrimp paste to form a fine paste. Keep aside.

3) Heat the peanut oil in a pan and fry the mushrooms until golden brown. Sprinkle a little salt and fish sauce to add flavour. Remove from heat.

4) Now add the coconut cream to the pan and heat until it begins to thicken.

5) Add the chilly paste to this and stir until the oil separates from the cream.

6) Flavour with the sugar and fish sauce and contine boiling until the sauce reduces to half.

7) *Add the shrimps and mix. Cook until done.*
8) *Finally add the mushrooms and garnish with cilantro sprigs.*
9) *Serve hot.*

Note:
- *Serve with steamed rice. You can replace the shrimps with the meat or vegetables of your choice.*

Lemongrass Chicken

Serves: 4

Cooking time (approx.): 20 minutes

(This excludes time for preparartion)

Ingredients:

Chicken thighs (boneless)	: 500 gms	Palm sugar	: 2 tbsp
Lemongrass stalks	: 2	Sea salt	: 1 tsp
Garlic cloves (minced)	: 3	Fish sauce	: 2 tbsp
Black pepper (ground)	: ¼ tsp	Peanut oil	: 4 tbsp
Thai chilly (ground)	: ½ tsp		

Procedure:

1) Wash the chicken thoroughly and cut into medium sized pieces.

2) Pound the lemongrass stalks using a mortar and pestle.

3) In a bowl, mix the lemongrass, chicken, garlic, bleck pepper, Thai chilly, sugar, salt and fish sauce and refrigerate for 2–3 hours.

4) Heat the peanut oil in a pan for about a minute. Put the marinated chicken and stir fry for 15 minutes, until the chicken and sauce caramelize.

To serve: Serve it with a cool cucumber salad.

Tip:

• Lemongrass is generally used only for flavouring, but in this Thai recipe, you can eat it as well.

Drunken Stir Fry

(Pad Kee Mao)

Serves: 4–6

Cooking time (approx.): 10 minutes

Ingredients:

Chicken breast (minced)	: 2 cups	White sugar	: 1 tsp
Garlic cloves (chopped)	: 15	Fish sauce	: 2tbsp
Coriander (chopped)	: 4 tsp	Oyster sauce	: 2 tbsp
Fresh holy basil	: ½ cup	Chicken stock	: ¼ cup
Red chilly (sliced)	: 2	Cooking oil	: 2 tbsp
Chilly peppers	: 5	Holy basil leaves for garnishing.	

Procedure:

1) Make a smooth paste of the chilly peppers, coriander and garlic.

2) In a pan, heat the oil and fry the coriander paste. To this, add the chicken.

3) Stir for 2 minutes. Now add white sugar, fish sauce, oyster sauce and chicken stock and bring to a boil.

4) When the dish begins to thicken, remove from heat and add the basil leaves and sliced red chilly. Mix well.

5) Garnish with holy basil leaves and serve.

Tip:

• As this dish is too hot, serve with a cold beer or whisky.

Thai stir–fried Chicken with Holy Basil

(Gai Pad Graprow)

Cooking time (approx.): 15 minutes

Ingredients:

Chicken thighs (boneless; chopped)	: 500 gms	Fish sauce	: 1–2 tbsp
Garlic cloves (chopped)	: 4–6	Holy basil	: 1 cup
Onion (sliced)	: ½ cup	Sweet basil	: 1 cup
Peanut oil	: 2–3 tbsp	Kaffir lime leaves	: 2
Black soy sauce	: 2 tsp	Chilies (chopped)	: 5–10
		White pepper (ground)	: 1 tsp

Procedure:

1) Heat oil in a pan and stir fry the onions and garlic until golden yellow.

2) Add the chicken and stir fry till it loses its pink colour.

3) To this, add the holy and sweet basil leaves, kaffir lime leaves and Chilies and stir again.

4) As the basil begins to cook, pour in the fish sauce, black soy sauce and white pepper powder.

To serve: Serve over a plate of steamed rice.

Tip:

• The smaller the chicken pieces, the better.

Barbecued Chicken with Dipping Sauce

(Gai Yang Sohng Kreuang)

Serves: 6

Cooking time (approx.): 25–30 minutes

(This excludes time for preparation)

Ingredients:

Chicken leg – thigh pieces	: 6	**For sauce:**	
Cilantro roots (chopped)	: 1 tbsp	Whole red hot Chilies	: 10–15
Garlic cloves (finely chopped)	: 8–10	Garlic	: 6–8
		White vinegar	: ¼ cup
Onions (finely chopped)	: 3	Lime juice	: 4–6 tsp
White pepper– corns (ground)	: 2 tsp	Fish sauce	: 4 tbsp
		Sugar	: ½ cup
Coriander seeds	: 1 tbsp	Green onion (finely chopped)	: 1"
Yellow curry powder	: 2 tsp		
Fish sauce	: 2–3 tbsp		section
Sugar	: 1 tsp		
Coconut milk	: ½ cup		

Procedure for Chicken:

1) Grind the cilantro roots, garlic and onions to make a paste.
2) To this add the white pepper powder, coriander seeds and curry powder and blend again.
3) Now add the fish sauce and sugar and mix to form a smooth paste.
4) Coat the chicken pieces generously with the paste and keep overnight for marination.
5) Grill the chicken pieces over hot charcoals turning frequently. Just before grilling, add the coconut milk to the paste.
6) Serve with the dipping sauce.

Procedure for Sauce:

1) Soak the red Chilies in water until softened (about 1 hour) and then chop.

2) *Make a fine paste of the garlic cloves.*
3) *Add the Chilies to the garlic paste.Blend together.*
4) *To this paste add vinegar, lime juice, fish sauce and sugar. Mix until the sugar dissolves.*
5) *Keep for 15 minutes.*
6) *Just before serving, garnish with spring onions.*

To serve: *Serve with steamed sticky rice and raw papaya salad.*

Fried Tofu with Garlic and Black Pepper

Serves: 3–4

Cooking time (approx.): 20 minutes

Ingredients:

Tofu (cut into small pieces)	: 400 gms	Sugar	: ½ tsp
Garlic cloves (smashed)	: 3	Vegetable oil	: 4 tbsp
Onions (peeled)	: 2–3	Cucumber slices, coriander	
Whole black peppercorns	: 1 tsp	leaves, tomatoes	: for
Soy sauce	: 2 tbsp		garnish

Procedure:

1) Grind the garlic, onions and peppercorns together to form a paste.

2) To this, add soy sauce and sugar and stir.

3) Marinate the tofu pieces with this mixture and keep overnight.

4) Heat oil in a pan and stir fry the marinated tofu until golden brown.

5) Garnish with cucumber, coriander leaves and tomatoes.

Stir Fried vegetables with Garlic, Ginger and Lime

Serves: 2–3

Cooking time (approx.): 20 minutes

Ingredients:

Medium sized		For the Stir fry Sauce:	
carrot (sliced)	: 1	Vegetable broth	: ¼ cup
Chinese cabbage	: 1 cup	Fish sauce	: 2 tbsp
Small red pepper	: 1	Lime juice	: 1 tbsp
Small green pepper	: 1	Garlic (minced)	: 5–7
Mushrooms	: 5–7	Honey	: 1 tsp
Spring onions	: 3	Corn starch (dissolved	
Small head broccoli	: 1	in water)	: 1 tsp
Ginger (sliced)	: 1" piece	Green chilly (minced)	: 1
		White wine	: 2–4 tbsp
		Peanuts, cashews as per taste	

Procedure:

1) Prepare the sauce first. Over medium heat in a pan, mix the broth, fish sauce, lime juice, honey and chilly.

2) Now add the garlic and corn starch, stirring continuously for about 30–45 seconds.

3) Simmer for 2 minutes. Flavour accordingly with peanuts and cashews.

4) Heat oil in a pan. Stir fry the carrots, ginger and mushrooms until soft.

5) Add the white wine as the pan becomes dry.

6) Now add the rest of the vegetables and stir .

7) Pour the stir fry sauce in the pan and mix well. Remove from heat.

8) When serving, serve atop a plate of steamed rice.

Tip:

• When stir–frying vegetables, fry the tough vegetables first, else the soft ones become soggy waiting for the tough ones to cook.

Thai style Stir Fried vegetables

Serves: 2–4

Cooking time (approx.): 15 minutes

Ingredients:

Green vegetables (cut)	: 2 cups	Soy sauce	: 2 tbsp
Garlic cloves (smashed)	: 2–3	Oyster sauce	: 2 tbsp
Vegetable oil	: 3 tbsp	Sugar	: ⅓ tsp
Fish sauce	: 1 tbsp	Water	: ¼ cup

Procedure:

1) Heat oil in a pan. Add garlic and stir.

2) Now add the vegetables and stir fry until they wilt.

3) Immediately add the fish sauce, soy sauce, oyster sauce, sugar and water.

4) Stir for 2–3 minutes. Remove from heat.

To serve: Serve hot.

Fried Noodles

(Pad Thai)

Serves: 4

Cooking time (approx.): 20 minutes

Ingredients:

Rice noodles (soaked)	: 4 cups	Chilly powder	: 1 tsp
Eggs	: 3	Ground roasted peanuts	: ½ cup
Tofu (diced)	: 50 gms	Coconut palm sugar	: 4 tbsp
Bean sprouts	: 250 gms	Fish sauce	: 3 tbsp
Chinese chives	: 50 gms	Vinegar	: 4 tbsp
Onion (chopped)	: 1 tbsp	Water	: ¼ cup
Garlic (chopped)	: 1 tbsp	Vegetable oil	: 8 tbsp
Salted chinese radish (chopped)	: 3 tbsp		

Procedure:

1) In a pan, stir fry the garlic and onions until golden yellow.

2) When done, add the noodles and water.

3) Now add sugar, fish sauce and vinegar to the noodles.

4) Move the noodles to one side of the pan and add 3 tbsp oil and put the tofu, chinese radish and chilly powder and saute.

5) Take this mixture also to the side and again put oil into the pan breaking the eggs into it. Also add the bean sprouts and chinese chives.

6) Now add the peanuts and mix everything together.

Tip:

• Garnish with fresh vegetables on top.

Sticky Rice

(Kao Ne – Ow)

Serves: 6

Cooking time (approx.): 35 minutes

(Excludes preparation time)

Ingredients:

Sticky rice	: 500 gms

Sticky rice steamer (a metal pot with bamboo steamer basket: an electric rice cooker won't give the same effect)

Procedure:

1) Soak the rice in water overnight. The rice will become double its size so use appropriate amount of water.

2) Drain and rinse the rice. In the metal pot, boil some water and place the bamboo steamer basket on top.

3) Place the rice in the basket and cover with a thick lid.

4) Steam for about 30–35 minutes.

Fried Rice with Chicken

(Kao Paht Gy)

Serves: 2

Cooking time (approx.): 15 minutes

Ingredients:

Chicken breast (small pieces)	: 250 gms	Light soy sauce	: 1 tsp
Vegetable oil	: 3 tbsp	Ground black pepper	: ¼ tsp
Fish sauce	: 1 tbsp	Sugar	: 1 tsp
Garlic clove (smashed)	: 1	Cucumber (peeled and sliced)	: 1
Cooked basmati rice	: 2 cups	Lime, fresh red Chilies	: as per taste
Egg (lightly beaten with ½ tsp water)	: 1		

Procedure:

1) Cook the chicken in a pan over medium flame for about 5 miutes.

2) Add ½ tbsp fish sauce to the chicken and stir. Remove from heat.

3) In another pan, heat some oil and stir fry the garlic until brown.

4) Add the rice to the pan and cook briefly.

5) Now add the chicken and mix well.

6) To this, add the soy sauce, fish sauce, egg, sugar, pepper, lime and red Chilies.

7) Mix all the ingredients together with a light hand, not letting the rice grains break.

8) Garnish with cucumber slices. Serve hot.

Coconut Rice

Serves: 4

Cooking time (approx.): 25 minutes

Ingredients:

Basmati rice	: 2 cups	Vegetable oil	: ½ tsp
Coconut milk	: 2 cups	Brown sugar	: 1 tsp
Water	: 2 cups	Shredded coconut	: 2 tsp
Salt	: ½ tsp		

Procedure:

1) Grease a deep–sided pot with oil.
2) Put the rice, coconut milk, water and salt in the pan.
3) Place the pan on a medium flame and mix the ingredients well.
4) Add the sugar and stir. Bring the contents to a boil.
5) Cover the pot with a lid, allowing a little heat to escape.
6) Steam for about 12–15 minutes.
7) Close the flame but don't remove from stove.
8) Cover the lid tightly and keep for 5 minutes. This will make it sticky.
9) Dry fry the shredded coconut in a pan and use for garnishing.

Tip:
- If using brown rice instead, double the amount of coconut milk.

Crispy Noodles in Sweet and Sour Sauce

(Mee Krob)

Serves: 2

Cooking time (approx.): 20 minutes

Ingredients:

Thin rice noodle vermicelli (soaked)	: ¾ cup	Palm sugar	: 4 tbsp
Chicken (finely chopped)	: ¼ cup	Ground dried Chilies	: 1 tsp
Fresh shrimp (finely chopped)	: ¼ cup	Tofu (cut and fried)	: 1 cake
Garlic and onion (finely chopped)	: 1 tbsp	Pickeled garlic bulbs (sliced)	: 2
Fermented soy beans	: 1 tbsp	Fresh chilly (sliced)	: 1
White vinegar	: 1 tbsp	Chinese chives	: 3
Fish sauce	: 1 tbsp	Fresh bean sprouts	: ⅔ cups
		Vegetable oil	: ¼ cups
		Kaffir lime rind (sliced)	: 1 tbsp

Procedure:

1) Take the oil in a pan and heat. Fry the garlic and onion until they become translucent.

2) Put the noodles in the pan and toss. Now flavour with the soy beans, vinegar, sugar, dried Chilies and fish sauce.

3) Add the chicken and shrimp and allow to cook for 5–10 minutes.

4) As the sauce begins to thicken, add vinegar. Mix well.

5) Now add the noodles, tofu, bean sprouts, chinese chives and fresh chilly. Mix with the sauce.

6) Garnish with kaffir lime rind and garlic bulbs.

Tip:

- Tastes best when served hot.

Sticky Rice with Mango

Serves: 2–3

Cooking time (approx.): 45 minutes

(Excludes preparation time)

Ingredients:

Sticky rice	: 2 cups	Sugar	: 2 tbsp
Coconut milk	: 1¼ cup	Ripe mangoes (peeled	
Salt	: ¼ tsp	and sliced)	: 2

Procedure:

1) Soak the rice for about 1–2 hours. Drain.
2) In a pan, put the rice, salt, sugar, coconut milk and water and bring to a boil stirring occasionally.
3) Simmer for about 10 minutes and remove from heat.
4) Keep aside for 5–7 minutes until it cools off a little.
5) Put the rice into a steamer and steam for 20 minutes.
6) After cooking, put the rice into small moulds.
7) For serving, de–mould the rice and spread a layer of mangoes on top.

Tip:
- You can substitute mangoes with the fruit of your choice.

Black Sticky Rice with Mango

(Kao Niow Dahm)

Serves: *2–3*

Cooking time (approx.): *45 minutes*

(Excludes preparation time)

Ingredients:

Whole grain black sticky rice	: 2 cups	Toasted sesame seeds	: 2 tbsp
Coconut milk	: 2 cups	Strawberries and mint leaves	: as per
Sugar	: ½ cup		taste
Salt	: ½ tsp		

Procedure:

1) Soak the rice in water overnight.

2) Put the rice in a steamer and add boiling water to it. Steam for 20 minutes.

3) Meanwhile, in a pan, heat the coconut milk, salt and sugar and make a sauce. Stir regularly to avoid lumps.

4) When the rice is cooked, take out of the steamer and pour half the sauce over the rice. Keep for 15–20 minutes.

5) Mould the rice into cups or bowls and decorate with sesame seeds, strawberries and mint leaves.

6) Before serving, add the remaining sauce on top to enhance flavour.

Tip:

• Serve at room temperature.

Grilled Coconut Cake

(Kanom Bah Bin)

Serves: 4

Cooking time (approx.): 45 minutes

Ingredients:

Sticky rice flour	: 1 cup	Fresh coconut (shredded)	: 2 cups
Rice flour	: ½ cup	Limestone water	: 1 cup
Granulated sugar	: 1 cup	Vanilla essence	: 1 tsp
Salt	: ¼ tsp	Peanut oil	: 2–3 tbsp
Egg	: 1 large		

Procedure:

1) Mix both the types of flour together along with the sugar and salt.

2) Knead with the egg, vanilla essence and limestone water.

3) Continue kneading until the dough becomes wet of the coconut cream.

4) Take some peanut oil and grease the inner side of the baking dish.

5) Evenly spread the mixture into the dish and bake in the oven at 350° F for 20 minutes.

6) Take out the cake and gloss the upper side with a beaten egg. Bake again for 10 minutes at 400° F.

7) Take out the cake and cut into small pieces.

8) Serve warm.